MW01242333

HAPPY PEOPLE =
HAPPY WORLD

*Prayers to Heal People
and The World*

VINCENT D'SOUZA

BALBOA.PRESS

A DIVISION OF HAY HOUSE

Balboa Press books may be ordered through booksellers or by contacting:

Balboa Press
A Division of Hay House
1663 Liberty Drive
Bloomington, IN 47403
www.balboapress.com.au
AU TFN: 1 800 844 925 (Toll Free inside Australia)
AU Local: (02) 8310 7086 (+61 2 8310 7086 from outside Australia)

Print information available on the last page.

ISBN: 978-1-9822-9211-9 (sc)
ISBN: 978-1-9822-9212-6 (e)

Balboa Press rev. date: 11/25/2021

Recitation of The Prayers

It is preferable to say only one prayer or a group of prayers, with all your heart and mind, than to say a few or lots of prayers mechanically. Please reflect on the meanings of the prayers and the words that comprise them.

Any prayer can be recited alone but it is preferable to prefix it with the Sign of the Cross and conclude it with a Glory Be.

1. The New Rosary: Sign of the Cross; Offer one's intentions; Recite the I AM Prayer followed by the Pardon, Petition and Commitment (PPC) prayer three times; The Glory Be; Affirmation 1. Announce the First Mystery. Recite the I AM Prayer, then the PPC prayer ten times, The Glory Be followed by the affirmation that corresponds to the mysteries. Repeat this for five, ten or fifteen mysteries. Conclude with It is Finished, followed by the Concluding Prayer of thanks and the Sign of the Cross.

2. The Seven Stations of the Healing Cross is to be recited as one wishes: daily; as a novena; weekly, etc.

3. The New Angelus: Recite In the morning only, morning and evening or the morning, midday and evening as you feel appropriate.

4. The Daily Invocation: As the name says.

5. The Healing Decrees: As you wish, but the Call to the Fire Breath preferably daily.

6. The Hail Mary and Holy Mary: These can be used in place of the PPC prayer.

Always have a Preamble and a Closure. Suggestions are given but you can make your own ones.

Contents

A Daily Invocation

May the infinite unconditional love from the heart of the
Creator God,
Saturate the hearts of all people, especially their leaders,
And manifest in all they think and feel.
I pray God's love guides all that I think and feel.

May the infinite knowledge and wisdom, from the mind of the
Creator God,
Penetrate the minds of all people, especially their leaders,
And manifest in all they say and do.
I pray God's wisdom guides all I say and do.

May the infinite peace and harmony, of the Spirit of the Creator God,
Reign in all people and all creation, especially their leaders,
And manifest in all they think, feel, say and do.
I pray God's peace guides all I think, feel, say and do.

May love, wisdom, peace and harmony, reign in all people and all
creation,
The call compels the answer, we reap what we sow,
Our choices create all that happens to us,
I pray love, wisdom, peace guide all to live in harmony.
Amen! Amen! Amen!

2

The New Rosary

Sign of the Cross: In the name I AM of the power of the Father-Mother God, the love of the Christ and the wisdom of the Holy Spirit, three aspects of the eternal Creator, blazing as a threefold flame in my eternal spirit I AM. Amen!

OPENING PRAYER: I BELIEVE

Beloved almighty, glorious and holy Creator God, I believe that I AM an eternal spiritual flame, of radiant love, from Your heart in the Great Central Sun, the source of all creation – the Alpha and Omega. I AM guided by Helios and Vesta the spiritual leaders of this solar system, who nurture me, to raise the level of my cosmic awareness and God consciousness.

I AM a pilgrim on Earth, following in the steps of the way-showers – the earthly manifestations of The Christ: Lao Tse, Krishna, Buddha, Jesus, Mohammed, Bahai'Ullah etc. towards my eternal freedom from the bondage of the illusions of the physical senses and matter. I AM serving all creation, while I purify my lower bodies of negative beliefs, by the power of the sacred fire, channelled through this body by my thoughts, feelings, words and deeds.

Every moment, the Divine Flame, The Spirit of God, I AM in my physical being, grows and expands, nurtured by the harmonising energies of the warmth and security of love, the power of peace and the healing energies of wisdom, all of which, transmute all the disharmonious foci of energy within my being. Daily, I manifest more of my oneness with God in my consciousness, direction, action and external manifestation.

Flooded with the light, love, omniscience and omnipresence of God, I continually manifest God's radiance by my smile, God's warmth by my unconditional love, God's wisdom by my choices, and God's power by my eternal peace, all of which perfect my lower bodies.

Hence, I AM achieving the ascension of my consciousness into the world of Spirit, where I will continue to serve God, after living a fruitful life on earth by practising God's will – promoting a creation of infinite love and harmony. Amen!

THE I AM (LORD'S) PRAYER

Beloved, almighty, glorious and holy Creator God of all, immanent in all Your creation, I AM Your child. I AM the instrument of Your will being done. I AM living on earth as I AM one with You in spirit. I AM sharing Your blessings with all Your creation. I AM forgiven by all creation in the measure in which I forgive all creation. I AM leading all creation away from temptation, I AM delivering all creation from the power of the evil one. I AM living a life of good conduct, love, truth, peace and selfless service towards all creation, in accordance with Your divine will, under Your grace, in a perfect way. Thy Spirit which I AM is the kingdom, power and glory in eternal, immortal manifestation. All this I AM, I AM, I AM. Amen!

PRAYER OF PARDON, PETITION AND COMMITMENT

Beloved, almighty, glorious and holy God, we humbly ask for, gratefully accept and joyfully thank You for the pardon of our sins. We praise You and ask and accept, that the world and all its peoples be saturated with the healing energies of love, forgiveness, peace and light.

In the name of The Christ, your eternal beloved child, we joyfully ask for, accept, and follow the guidance of all spirits, incarnate or not, who lead us to practice unconditional love, forgiveness and sharing, towards ourselves and all creation, till our victory over the illusions of sin, disease and death, manifests our oneness in Spirit, God. I AM love, health, abundance, joy, appreciation, gratitude and peace to all. Amen!

THE HAIL MARY AND THE HOLY MARY

Hail Mary, the Lord is with thee, blessed art thou amongst women, and blessed is the fruit of thy womb, Jesus.

Holy Mary, mother of God, pray for us the children of God, now and till the hour of our victory, over the illusions of sin, disease and death.

GLORY BE

Glory be to the power of the Father-Mother God, the love of the children (the Christ), the wisdom of the Holy Spirit, three aspects of the Creator, blazing as a threefold flame in my eternal spirit. Almighty I AM! Almighty I AM! Almighty I AM! Amen!

AFFIRMATIONS

Affirmation 1: Recite at the end of the first triplet and decate of the New Rosary.

I use the love, wisdom and the power of God, my eternal spiritual Self, I AM, to heal and bring peace to all people and the world. Amen!

Affirmation 2: Recite after each Joyful Mystery triplet and decate.

Spirit of God I AM in me, I joyfully accept and follow Your guidance in my thoughts, feelings, words and deeds, which help me to live according to the Creator's will, to make earth a paradise once more. Amen!

Affirmation 3: Recite after each sorrowful mystery triplet and decate.

May all our mental, physical and emotional power be used for the good of all. May the love of The Christ heal and bring peace to all peoples. May our wisdom heal and bring joy to the world through our thoughts, feelings, words and deeds. Amen!

Affirmation 4: Recite after each Glorious Mystery triplet and decate.

I love, approve and allow, and care for myself, all people and the world. Amen!

CLOSING PRAYER: IT IS FINISHED!

It is Finished! Having reached the end of my mortal life, I manifest my spiritual immortality, and I again affirm my oneness with God, Spirit. I am aware of the wonder, beauty, harmony, unity and order in all of creation, including myself. I AM overjoyed to have been permitted to partake in all the manifestations of God, the All in all. Almighty, glorious and holy Creator, I know that Your angel thoughts, Your infinite love and Your Children, incarnate or not, reassure me when I feel alone, and lead me through positive ideas, encouragement and love, to fulfill Your divine will of love and harmony in all creation. My cup overflows with goodness and virtue; Your divine presence I AM that I AM, nurtures, guides and blesses me always.

I AM Your Spirit and love in action everywhere. I AM one with You and all creation both living and nonliving. I lift up the downtrodden and temper the pride of the wealthy, exhorting all, to seek their real true eternal selves, Your Spirit I AM in each of us. I bring peace to all, through freedom from the false bondage of human sensuality.

It is finished! I Am Your immortal, lovely, pure and victorious spirit – The Christ in action – seeking, through the mercy and compassion of eternal love, to save those spirits who are lost, through the distractions of matter and the physical senses.

It is finished! I AM eternal spirit, life, truth and Christ love, unaffected by death, and dedicated to free the world through the blessing of the ascension of the human consciousness, from a focus on temporal material manifestation, to a life of eternal harmony in Spirit, the Creator.

It is Finished! Daily my beloved holy Christself perfects my lower bodies, revealing my perfection and oneness with Your being, The Christ, the Holy Spirit and all of creation, till the moment, when I too can say with immortal love, "It is finished!"

Glory be

MYSTERIES OF THE ROSARY

The Joyful Mysteries represent:

Aspirations, nurturing and fulfilment; Qualities of the Feminine; The parent; The example.

The Sorrowful mysteries represent:

Choices, trials/lessons, distractions and surrender; Qualities of the Masculine; The child; Imitation of the example.

The Glorious Mysteries represent:

Harmonious union of the Masculine and the Feminine; The Adult; The result of the preparation in the other two groups of mysteries.

The first three of these mysteries, signify the achievement of unconditional love of oneself and all humanity – there is only one of all in God! The last two signify love, gratitude and peace within oneself and towards all of creation. The whole set signifies the pure, unconditional love of God the All in all and the All that is!

THE MEANING OF THE MYSTERIES

THE JOYFUL MYSTERIES

1. The Anunciation: The desire, the choice and the decision, to set and achieve a goal, eg have a child, learn something new, or help someone and face the consequences of the decision. Commitment and Acceptance.
2. The visitation: Share the choice or decision with others and enlist their support. Sharing and Support.
3. The Birth: Do the necessary to achieve the goal. Example: Getting a qualification or having a baby. Realisation.
4. The presentation: Perfect the product or talent or raise the child and offer it to the world, the temple of all humanity. Implementation.
5. The Finding in the Temple: Enjoy the satisfaction of the fruits of one's efforts. Joy and Gratitude.

THE SORROWFUL MYSTERIES:

1. Agony in the Garden: Decisions to face and surmount fears of failure. Decision making.
2. The Scourging at the Pillar: Doubts, peer pressure, teasing, negative advice. Doubts and fears.
3. The Crowning with Thorns: Trials, errors, ridicule, criticisms. Tests of the ego.
4. The Carrying of the Cross: Perseverance in spite of all the tests. Fortitude.

5. The Crucifixion and Death: Surrender of the material and mortal to enter the spiritual, real and eternal. Surrender/Death of the ego or false self.

THE GLORIOUS MYSTERIES:

1. The Resurrection: Awakening into the eternal perfection of Spirit. Birth into Spirit.
2. The Ascension: Elevation of consciousness; emphasis on love, truth and peace. Enter the Christ consciousness.
3. The Descent of the Spirit: Assistance to others on the path behind us. Raising the conscious awareness of others by vibration and example. Practising unconditional love.
4. The Assumption: Recognition of our debt to all creation, especially Mother Earth. Gratitude.
5. Coronation in Heaven: Living in harmony with all creation through unconditional love, wisdom and peace. Crowning the Spirit of the Earth in our minds – We are one with God and all. Oneness.

IF THE CHOICES AND THE FOCUS ARE POSITIVE,
THE RESULTS ARE POSITIVE AND VICE-VERSA!

WE REAP WHAT WE SOW! AMEN!

3

The New Angelus

1. The angel of the Lord declared unto me!

Prayer of affirmation:

And I conceived my Christself through the Holy Spirit! Through my Christ Consciousness, I see my oneness with all creation, the manifestation of God the All in all. I AM Spirit, Principle, Life, Truth, Love, Power, Mastery, Control, Wisdom, Obedience, Harmony, Gratitude, Justice, Reality, Vision and Victory! Amen!

2. Behold you are a child of God!

Prayer of affirmation:

Be it done unto me according to thy word!

3. And the Word was made flesh!

Prayer of affirmation:

And the Christ Consciousness dwells in my body and I follow its guidance!

4.   Pray for us the mother of God and all God's children!

Prayer of affirmation:

That we may be made worthy of the promises of The Christ!

Pour forth we beseech Thee and accept o God Thy grace into our hearts, that we to whom the incarnation of The Christ was made known by the message of an angel, may, by following and living its guidance be brought to the glory of the resurrection, and our ascension to our oneness with Thee, through the same Christ our Lord. Amen!

4

The Healing Decrees

PREAMBLE AND CLOSURE (SUGGESTED)

PREAMBLE: Covers intention and invitation of other light beings to help realize the intention.

In the name of the beloved presence of God I AM in me, in the name of my own beloved Holy Christ Self, I AM calling to the heart of the Saviour Jesus Christ and the servant sons of God and the legions of light, who are with him in heaven: By and through the magnetic power of the sacred fire vested in the three fold flame of love, wisdom and power burning within the secret chamber of my heart, I decree:-[1]

CLOSURE: This concludes the decreeing and gives thanks for the assistance and acceptance of the outcome in the present.

And in full faith, I consciously accept this manifest, manifest, manifest, (3x) right here and now, with full power, eternally sustained, all powerfully active, ever expanding, world, *universe and cosmos* enfolding, until all are wholly ascended in the light and free! Beloved I AM! Beloved I AM! Beloved I AM![1] *And so it is!*

---

[1]   Kuthumi and Djwalkul, dictated to Mark L. Prophet and Elizabeth C. Prophet, 1996. The Human Aura, pp 117-118, Summit University Press USA. *Italics are my insertion.*

CALL TO THE FIRE BREATH

Preamble

I AM, I AM, I AM the fire breath of God
From the heart of beloved Alpha and Omega.
This day I Am the immaculate concept
In expression everywhere I move.
Now I AM full of joy
For now I AM the full expression
Of divine love.
My beloved I AM Presence,
Seal me now in the very heart of
The expanding fire breath of God.
Let its purity, wholeness, and love
Manifest everywhere I AM today and forever! (recite three times)

I accept this done right now with full power!
I AM this done right now with full power!
I AM, I AM, I AM God Life expressing perfection
All ways at all times.
This which I call forth for myself'
I call forth for every man, woman and child
On this planet.[1]

Closure

HEART, HEAD AND HAND DECREE

Preamble

Heart

---

[1]   Kuthumi and Djwalkul, dictated to Mark L. Prophet and Elizabeth C. Prophet, 1996. The Human Aura, pp 206-207, Summit University Press USA.

Violet Fire, thou Love divine,
Blaze within this heart of mine,
Thou art Mercy forever true,
Keep me always in tune with you. (Recite three times)

Head
I AM light thou Christ in me,
Set my mind forever free,
Violet Fire, forever shine,
Deep within this mind of mine. (Recite 3 times)

God who gives my daily bread,
With Violet Fire
Fill my head,
Till Thy radiance heavenlike,
Makes my mind a mind of Light. (Recite three times)

Hand
I AM the hand of God in action,
Gaining victory every day;
My pure soul's great satisfaction
Is to walk the Middle Way.[1] (Recite three times)

Closure

TUBE OF LIGHT DECREE

Preamble

Beloved I AM Presence bright,
Round me seal Your Tube of Light
From ascended master flame
Called forth now in God's own name.

---

[1]   Kuthumi and Djwalkul, dictated to Mark L. Prophet and Elizabeth C. Prophet, 1996. The Human Aura, pp 22, Summit University Press USA.

13

Let it keep my temple free
From all discord sent to me.

I AM calling forth Violet Fire
To blaze and transmute all desire,
Keeping on in Freedom's name
Till I AM one with the Violet Flame.[1] (recite both verses three times)

Closure

FORGIVENESS DECREE

I AM Forgiveness acting here
Casting out all doubt and fear,
Setting men (*people*) forever free
With wings of cosmic Victory.

I AM calling in full power
For Forgiveness every hour;
To all life in every place
I flood forth forgiving Grace.[2] (recite both verses three times)

Closure

I AM LIGHT DECREE
(for strengthening the Aura)

Preamble

I AM Light, glowing Light,
Radiating Light, intensified Light.
God consumes my darkness,

---

[1]   Kuthumi and Djwalkul, dictated to Mark L. Prophet and Elizabeth C. Prophet, 1996. The Human Aura, pg 23, Summit University Press USA.

[2]   Kuthumi and Djwalkul, dictated to Mark L. Prophet and Elizabeth C. Prophet, 1996. The Human Aura, pp 23, Summit University Press USA.

Transmuting it into Light.
This day I AM a focus of the Central Sun.
Flowing through me is a crystal river,
A living fountain of Light
That can never be qualified
By human thought or feeling.

I AM an outpost of the Divine.
Such darkness that has used me is swallowed up
By the mighty river of Light which I AM.

I AM, I AM, I AM Light;
I live, I live, I live in Light.
I AM Light's fullest dimension;
I AM Light's purest intention.

I AM Light, Light, Light,
Flooding the world everywhere I move,
Blessing, strengthening and conveying
The purpose of the kingdom of heaven.[1]

Closure

SELF PURIFICATION DECREES

Preamble

I AM a gigantic pillar of Violet Consuming Fire, that transcends all human concepts, and showers constantly all the triumph and perfection of the Creator God.

---

[1]   Kuthumi and Djwalkul, dictated to Mark L. Prophet and Elizabeth C. Prophet, 1996. The Human Aura, pp 45, Summit University Press USA.

Beloved Presence of God I AM in me, apply Your Violet Transmuting Flame to me, so that it transmutes all my errors and defects, past and present, their cause and effect, and dissolves all my problems forever.

Beloved Presence of God, I AM, in me, apply Your Violet Transmuting Flame to me, so that it transmutes everything contrary to health, wellbeing and peace in me and all that surrounds me. Seal me in a channel of light and energy, as an impenetrable wall, against which, all negative forces, internal or external impinge, and return to their source transmuted into peace, love, wellbeing and abundance, for the benefit of all those it reaches in its action.

Blaze the Violet Transmuting Flame through my Feeling body. Dissolve and transmute all feelings of doubt, fear, imperfection, anger, and replace them with feelings of divine love, Self-worth, peace, purity and okeness.

Blaze the Violet Transmuting Flame through my Mental body. Dissolve and transmute all thoughts of ugliness, low esteem, doubt and failure and replace them with thoughts of high esteem, beauty, success, self-confidence and courage.

Blaze the Violet Transmuting Flame through my Etheric body. Dissolve and transmute all memories of pain and hurt, discord and violence, failure and limitation, and replace them with memories of success, capability, harmony, joy, gratitude and peace.

Blaze the Violet Transmuting Flame through every cell, organ and function of my physical body. Sustain it there until all manifestation of disease, aging and any other imperfection, is dissolved and transmuted into my eternal youth and beauty, my perfect, vibrant, joyful and grateful health, and the victory and fulfilment of my role in the Divine Plan with Peace, Awareness, Love, Service and Joy and deep Gratitude. Thank You! And so it is!

Closure!

5

The Seven Stations of The Healing Cross

Welcome to this Prayer Meeting of THE SEVEN STATIONS OF THE HEALING CROSS.

OPENING HYMN: LORD OF INFINITE LOVE

Lord of infinite love, spirit, truth, life principle,
You're omnipotent, You're omniscient, You're all present, the All in all,
I'm You're image and likeness, You made me, hence I'm Your child,
I do Your will, love and forgive, and serve all.

Chorus
I love only You, I worship only You
I follow only You, please show me the way home,
I praise You and thank You
For the teachings I've encountered on the way.

You're My Father I'm Your child, like The Christ I do Your will,
I share my wares, love and forgive all Your creation
I choose my thoughts, all my feelings, all my words and all my deeds,
To promote love, truth and peace in all the world.

17

Chorus
Coda after the Chorus
You're my God, and I love You, in every way!

OPENING PRAYER

Beloved almighty, glorious and holy, Creator God, present in all Your creation, in the Name of Jesus The Christ, I/We invite all Your spiritual children, incarnate or not, to join me/us to pray for the manifestation of Your spiritual perfect design, in all our bodies and Mother Earth. We believe as Jesus promised us that He is present in our midst. I/We welcome Jesus here. We also invite and welcome to this prayer meeting, The Holy Spirit – the Comforter – our universal mother, the blessed virgin Mary, all the angels and saints, and all those who have done Your will throughout the ages. We respect the divine will and the will of every person in our prayers.

THE KEEPERS DAILY PRAYER[1]

A Flame is active; A Flame is vital; A Flame is eternal. I AM a God Flame of radiant love from the very Heart of God in the Great Central Sun, descending from the Master of Life! I AM charged now with beloved Helios and Vesta's Supreme God Consciousness and Solar Awareness.

Pilgrim upon earth, I AM walking daily the way of the Ascended Masters' victory that leads to my eternal freedom by the power of the Sacred Fire, this day and always, continually made manifest in my thoughts, feelings and immediate awareness, transcending and transmuting all the elements of earth within my four lower bodies, and freeing me by the power of the Sacred Fire from those misqualified foci of energy within my being.

---

[1]   Prophet M L & E C *My Soul Doth Magnify the Lord,* pp 135-137, 1986, Summit University Press, USA

I AM set free right now from all that binds, by and through the currents of the Divine Flame, of the Sacred Fire itself, whose ascending action makes me God in manifestation, God in action, God by direction and God in consciousness!

I Am an active Flame! I AM a vital Flame! I Am an eternal Flame! I Am an expanding Fire Spark from the Great Central Sun, drawing to me now every ray of divine energy which I need, and which can never be requalified by the human, and flooding me with the Light and God-illumination of a thousand suns, to take dominion and rule supreme forever, everywhere I AM!

Where I AM there God is also. Unseparated forever I remain, increasing my Light by the smile of His radiance, the fullness of His love, the omniscience of His wisdom, and the power of His life eternal, which automatically raises me on ascension's wings of victory, that shall return me to the Heart of God, from whence in truth I AM come to do God's will and manifest abundant life to all.

1. THE FIRST STATION OF THE HEALING CROSS

THE CROSS OF LOVE AND FORGIVENESS

Beloved, almighty, glorious and holy Creator God. Your Son Jesus The Christ commanded us to love and forgive – to trust You to care for us in every circumstance, and to provide for us, just as you do for the lilies of the field and the birds of the air. Hence, we carry the Cross of Love and Forgiveness before You and we declare our unconditional love for You and all people, from every atom, molecule and cell of our beings and our unconditional forgiveness of ourselves, all people, and all Your creation. We pray for our total forgiveness and for us to see the light and follow it to Your heart.

We release all negative energies of fear, based on illusions of imperfection in our minds, our bodies, or our lives to the purifying fires of God, Spirit, to be transmuted into Love, Truth, Life, Peace and Gratitude.

Beloved Jesus The Christ, through the Cross of Love and Forgiveness, thanks for guiding us all to walk on the waters with faith, through an understanding of Your teachings, without any doubt in our hearts, like Simon Peter on the lake. We humbly accept that the wills of God and all spiritual beings be done as a consequence of our prayers. You taught us that if we ask, believing that we have received, we will receive. Hence we pray and thank our Father in Heaven for healing His children and the Earth, by dispelling all illusions of imperfection from their beings. Children of God and the Earth you are healed! Thank You Father! And so it is!

All affirm: We submit ourselves to the care of God and Jesus The Christ. May God's will be done!

All recite an I AM Prayer, Hail Mary and Glory Be.

2.   THE SECOND STATION OF THE HEALING CROSS

THE CROSS OF PARDON

Beloved, almighty, glorious and holy, Creator God, we Your children come before you with the Cross of Pardon, and humbly confess: We have at times, by intention or omission, misused Your graces through our thoughts, feelings, words or deeds, against ourselves, other people, or the rest of Your creation. From every atom, molecule and cell of our beings, we repent of these actions. We resolve to choose only those thoughts, feelings, words and deeds that promote only love and forgiveness in all of creation and manifest the perfection of our spiritual selves, made in Your image and likeness. Father we humbly ask for, accept and thank You for Your pardon.

Beloved Jesus The Christ, through the Cross of Pardon, we ask You to guide us on The Way, The Truth and The Life, as "we forgive those who trespass against us" unconditionally. We pray for them and ourselves as You did on Calvary – Father forgive us for we know not what we do! Thank You! Please let these efforts and our conscious choices of thoughts, feelings, words and deeds, that fulfill Your commandment of universal love, dispel all negative energies, which generate illusions of imperfection in our minds and our physical bodies. Hence, our true, real and eternal spiritual perfection, as God's image and likeness, can manifest through healings in our physical bodies and harmony in our material lives. This, we believe is the Father's will being done. Children of God and the Earth you are healed! Thank You Father! And so it is!

All affirm: We submit ourselves to the care of God and Jesus The Christ. May God's will be done!

All recite the I AM Prayer, Hail Mary and Glory be.

3.   THE THIRD STATION OF THE HEALING CROSS

THE CROSS OF ACCEPTANCE AND GRATITUDE

Beloved almighty, glorious and holy, Creator God, we Your children come before You with The Cross of Acceptance and Gratitude. We accept the pardon You have granted us through Your Infinite, Eternal, Love. From every atom, molecule and cell of our beings, we are grateful for Your pardon. We forgive and love ourselves and all people. We now manifest the perfection of our spiritual selves, made in Your image and likeness.

Beloved Jesus The Christ; You commanded us, when You said," Be ye perfect as your Father in heaven is perfect!" Thanks for helping all of us, the children of God and all here present, to believe in our hearts that we are perfect, because we are made in God's image and likeness. In God there is no error and therefore disease is impossible. Hence, disease is impossible in any of us. It is an illusion of imperfection created by mortal mind. Children of God and the Earth you are healed. Thank You Father! And so it is!

All affirm: We submit ourselves to the care of God and Jesus The Christ. May God's will be done!

All recite an I AM Prayer, Hail Mary and Glory be.

4.   THE FOURTH STATION OF THE HEALING CROSS

THE CROSS OF HEALING

Beloved, almighty, glorious and holy, Creator God. We Your children in Spirit, clothed in our lower bodies, come before You with The Cross of Healing. Overflowing with love and forgiveness for all creation, both living and nonliving; pardoned and purified by Your pure love; full of gratitude for all Your blessings; every atom, molecule and cell of our lower bodies manifest the perfection of our spiritual selves made in Your image and likeness. We are healed in our Mental, Etheric, Emotional and Physical bodies.

Beloved Jesus The Christ; we believe that you are present in our midst and our hearts. We humbly ask You to say the word so that all of us and the Earth may be healed; that through Your gesture of pure love and our healing, God may be glorified, in our hearts in our words and in our lives. Children of God and the Earth you are healed. Thank You Father! And so it is!

All affirm: We submit ourselves to the care of God and Jesus The Christ. May God's will be done!

All recite an I AM Prayer, Hail Mary and Glory be.

5.   THE FIFTH STATION OF THE HEALING CROSS

THE CROSS OF THE JOY OF THE RESURRECTION

Beloved almighty, glorious and holy Creator God, we your children come before You with the Cross of the Joy of the Resurrection. We lift all our thoughts, feelings, words and deeds, above the illusions of imperfection in ourselves, others and all Your creation. All is in divine order full of principle, spirit, life, love and peace. From every atom, molecule and cell of our beings, our minds and our emotions, we resolve to see and affirm Your love, perfection and order in everything.

Beloved Jesus The Christ; During Your mission You taught us: "You can do what I can do and even greater things than these." Hence, we command in the name of Jesus The Christ, that all evil spirits and all illusions of imperfection, sin, disease or death depart from the bodies of all God's children and the Earth and we see them perfect as our Father in heaven is perfect. Children of God and the Earth you are healed. Thank You Father! And so it is!

All affirm: We submit ourselves to the care of God and Jesus The Christ. May God's will be done!

All recite an I AM Prayer a Hail Mary and a Glory be.

6.   THE SIXTH STATION OF THE HEALING CROSS

THE CROSS OF THE GLORY OF THE ASCENSION

Beloved almighty, glorious and holy, Creator God, we your children in spirit, love and truth, come before You with the Cross of the Glory of the Ascension. Healed of our illusions of imperfection, and having joyously risen above all temptation, we ascend into the glory of our spiritual selves, made in Your image and likeness. We are Eternal principle, love, truth, life and peace, doing Your will, by sowing love, truth and harmony in all creation.

Beloved Jesus The Christ: You taught us "Know the truth and it will set you free!". Like the lady who was healed of a twelve year haemorrhage by touching your garment of truth in faith, all God's children represented in these prayers, touch your garment of truth with faith, believing that they are healed. May our faith, based on the understanding of our spiritual perfection, permit the virtue of spirit to manifest in our healing. Children of God and the Earth you are healed. Thank You Father! And so it is!

All affirm: We submit ourselves to the care of God and Jesus The Christ. May God's will be done!

All recite an I AM Prayer, a Hail Mary and a Glory be.

7.   THE SEVENTH STATION OF THE HEALING CROSS

THE CROSS OF THE GLORIFICATION AND THE ADORATION OF THE CREATOR GOD

Beloved almighty, glorious and holy,Creator God, we Your children come before you, with the Cross of the Glorification and Adoration of Your being. In full recognition of our spiritual perfection, having transmuted all illusions of imperfection in our lower bodies, led by Jesus The Christ and our universal mother the blessed virgin Mary, we come before you with infinite love, gratitude and joy. We adore and glorify You in ourselves, all people and all Your creation. With all the heavenly hosts we sing: HOLY! HOLY! HOLY! GOD OF POWER AND LOVE! HEAVEN AND EARTH ARE FULL OF YOUR GLORY, HOSANNAH IN THE HIGHEST! BLESSED ARE ALL WHO DO YOUR HOLY WILL IN YOUR HOLY NAME **I AM**, HOSANNAH IN THE HIGHEST!

Beloved Jesus The Christ and beloved Mary our virgin mother; together with You, purified, perfect, and present in spirit before the Father, we command our spirits and the spirit of the Earth TALITA CUMI! That it may make our mortal minds wake up from the sleep of the mortal illusions of sin, disease or death to the reality of our eternal spiritual perfection and life as the image and likeness of God. Children of God and the Earth you are healed. Thank You Father! And so it is!

All affirm: We submit ourselves to the care of God and Jesus The Christ. May God's will be done!

All recite an I AM Prayer, a Hail Mary and a Glory be.

IT IS FINISHED

"It is finished! Done with this episode in strife, I AM made one with immortal Life. Calmly I AM resurrecting my spiritual energies from the great treasure house of immortal knowing.

The days I knew with Thee, O Father, before the world was – the days of triumph, when all the thoughts of Thy Being soared over the ageless hills of cosmic memory, come again as I meditate upon Thee. Each day as I call forth Thy memories from the scroll of immortal Love, I AM thrilled anew. Patterns wondrous to behold enthrall me with the wisdom of Thy creative scheme. So fearfully and wonderfully am I made, that none can mar Thy design, none can despoil the beauty of Thy holiness, none can discourage the beating of my heart, in almost wild anticipation of Thy fullness made manifest within me.

O great and glorious Father, how shall a tiny bird created in hierarchical bliss elude Thy compassionate attention? I AM of greater value than many birds, and therefore do I know, that Thy loving thoughts, reach out to me each day, to console me in seeming aloneness, to raise my courage, elevate my concepts, exalt my character, flood my being with virtue and power, sustain Thy cup of Life flowing over within me, and abide within me forever in the Nearness of Thy heavenly Presence.

I cannot fail, because I AM Thyself in action everywhere. I ride with Thee upon the mantle of the clouds. I walk with Thee upon the waves and crests of waters abundance. I move with Thee in the undulations of Thy currents, passing over the thousands of hills composing earth's crusts. I AM alive with Thee in each bush, flower and blade of grass. All nature sings in Thee and me, for we are one. I AM alive in the hearts of the downtrodden, raising them up. I AM the Law exacting the Truth of Being in the hearts of the proud, debasing the human creation therein and spurring the search for Thy Reality. I AM all things of bliss to all people of peace. I AM the full facility of divine grace, the Spirit of Holiness, releasing all hearts from bondage into unity.

It is finished! Thy perfect creation is within me, immortally lovely, it cannot be denied the blessedness of Being. Like unto Thyself it abides in the House of Reality. Nevermore to go out into profanity, it knows only the wonders of purity and victory. Yet there stirs within this immortal fire, a consummate pattern of mercy and compassion, seeking to save forever that which is lost, through wandering away from the beauty of reality and truth. I AM the living Christ in action evermore!

It is finished! Death and human concepts have no power in my world! I AM sealed by God design, with the fullness of that Christ-love, that overcomes, transcends, and frees the world by the power of the three times three, until all the world is God-victorious ascended in the light and free.

It is finished! Completeness is the allness of God. Day unto day an increase in strength, devotion, life, beauty and holiness occurs within me, released from the fairest flower of my Being, the Christ-consecrated rose of Sharon, unfolding its petals within my heart. My heart is the Heart of God! My heart is the Heart of the world! My heart is the Heart of Christ in healing action! Lo I AM with you always, even unto the end, when with the Voice of Immortal Love, I too shall say **"It is finished!"**[1]

---

[1]   Prophet M. L. and E. C. *My Soul Doth Magnify the Lord!* Summit Press, 1986, pp 139-142.

CONCLUDING PRAYER

Beloved, almighty, glorious and holy Creator God, we Your children joyfully and gratefully thank You, The Holy Spirit, The Comforter beloved Jesus The Christ, our universal mother The blessed virgin Mary, all the angels and saints and all our brothers and sisters, who have done Your will throughout the ages, for your love, guidance and protection, in our lives and in all creation; for our forgiveness, purification and healing in this service; for joining us in this service, and we join with them to sing Your unending hymn of praise: HOLY! HOLY! HOLY! GOD OF POWER AND LOVE! HEAVEN AND EARTH ARE FULL OF YOUR GLORY! HOSANNAH IN THE HIGHEST! BLESSED ARE ALL WHO DO YOUR HOLY WILL IN YOUR HOLY NAME **I AM**! HOSANNAH IN THE HIGHEST!

We now depart to love, honour and serve You in all Your creation, by practicing unconditional love, sharing and forgiveness. Thank You Father! And so it is!

CLOSING HYMN

I AM SPIRIT, I AM FREE!
Or Psalm 23

"There's no life, truth, intelligence, nor substance in matter,
All is Infinite Mind and its infinite manifestation,
For God is All in all.
Spirit is immortal truth, matter is mortal error,
Spirit is the real and eternal, matter is unreal and temporal.
Spirit is God, and man is God's image and likeness,
Therefore man is not material he is spiritual!"[1]
So be ye perfect as your Father in heaven is perfect

---

[1] Baker Eddy Mary, *Science and Health with Key to the Scriptures,* First Church of Christ scientist publishers, p468, 1875

You can do what I can do and even more!
Know the truth, and it will, set you free!

I AM Spirit, I AM perfect, image and likeness of the Creator
Matter conforms to my decrees.
I work with forgiveness, love and truth in all creation
Hence, sin does not exist in me.
I AM one with the Christ, the eternal child of God.
I AM one with the Creator, the Creator's one with me!
I was born to do the Creators will,
To sow love, truth and harmony
In all creation, both living and nonliving,
I joyfully do what I came to do!
I AM Spirit, Love and Truth, I AM free!

SIGN OF THE CROSS

6

The Litany of The Christ

Start and finish The Litany of The Christ with the Preamble and Closure suggested for the declaration of the Decrees of the Violet Flame.

Please note: **The Christ** is **Divine Love** in a mortal form; All living beings including **All** people all things and all no things or energetic forms, that are not visible or sensed by our five senses, are expressions of Divine or God's love.

Please be aware that as the name of God is **I AM,** according to Exodus in the Bible. So every time anyone says I AM......, they are really saying the spirit of God that I AM in this body I am using is .... whatever they state. You are the essence or the real, infinite and eternal part of the temporary expressions like the body or the ego mind that end when the body dies. You assert your divine nature in this litany, when you confirm **I AM that I AM!** because, your real nature is not the physical mortal body or the ego based human mind but the divine Mind (notice divine Mind is with a capital M while human mind has a small m, just as self with a small s is for the human self while Self with a capital S is for your real divine Self) which has all the qualities of God, the original Creator, that is infinite and eternal without form. You ensure that your brain, which is the computer that runs your body gets the message by stating for the first couplet of each pair of affirmations of the litany when you breathe in "I AM apart from this body, I AM ....!" And on the outbreath " I AM apart from this mind, I AM ....!"

For example: As you breathe in "I AM apart from this body, I AM a Christ!" and as you breathe out "I AM apart from this mind, I AM dimensionless!"

OK! Let us recite it!
Start with the Preamble.

Left column on the inbreath.	Right column on the outbreath.
Prefix: I Am apart from this body!	Prefix: I Am apart from this mind!
I Am a Christ!	I Am dimensionless!
I Am spirit!	I Am awareness!
I Am infinite!	I Am eternal!
I Am consciousness!	I Am allness!
I Am one with the All in all!	I Am one with the All that is!
I Am one with Source!	I Am one with God!
I Am free of all resistance!	I Am allowing all goodness to come to me!
I Am free of all doubt!	I Am worthy of receiving all goodness!
I Am free of worry and concern!	I Am trusting the universe to provide my needs!
I Am overflowing joy!	I Am the deepest gratitude!
I Am loved!	I Am loving!
I Am lovable!	I Am lovable forever!
I Am opening!	I Am allowing!
I Am receiving!	I Am taking in and grateful for God's bestowing!
I Am desire!	I Am intention!
I Am allowing!	I Am surrendered to the greatest good for all!
I Am peace!	I Am awareness!
I Am love and light!	I Am selfless service to all!
I Am joy!	I Am appreciation!

I Am gratitude!

I Am silence!

I Am oneness!

I Am!

I Am omniscience!

I Am omnipresence!

I Am one with every being!

I Am infinite!

I Am!

I Am truth!

I Am a part of divine justice!

I Am vibration!

I Am rhythm!

I Am cause and effect!

I Am intuition!

I Am mastery!

I Am a chooser!

I Am sound! (I decree!)

I Am worthy of good!

I Am generous!

I Am empathy!

I Am patience!

I Am humility!

I Am respect!

I Am health!

I Am allowance!

I Am joy!

I Am freedom!

I Am direction!

I Am clarity!

I Am forgiveness!

I Am allowance!

I Am joy!

I Am peace!

I Am stillness!

I Am beingness!

I Am That I AM!

I Am omnipotence!

I Am silence!

I Am one with everything and no thing!

I Am eternal!

I Am That I AM!

I Am wisdom!

I Am a part of divine mind!

I Am polarity!

I Am correspondence!

I Am generation!

I Am vision!

I Am a creator!

I Am a doer!

I Am light!

I Am abundance!

I Am discernment!

I Am compassion!

I Am praise!

I Am strength!

I Am forgiveness!

I Am service!

I Am acceptance!

I Am peace!

I Am focus!

I Am decisiveness!

I Am compassion!

I Am patience!

I Am understanding!

I Am enthusiasm!

I Am perspicacious!

I Am commitment!

I Am positive preferences!

I Am joyful preferences!

I Am peaceful preferences!

I Am contentment!

I Am knowledge!

I Am love!

I Am overflowing abundance!

I Am appreciation!

I Am peace!

I Am ecstasy!

I Am loved!

I Am lovable!

I Am one with God!

I Am the spirit of God in this body!

I Am doing nothing only by my mortal self!

I Am peace!

I Am love and light!

I Am courage!

I Am action!

I Am eager preferences!

I Am trusting preferences!

I Am grateful preferences!

I Am passion!

I Am empowerment!

I Am creative expression!

I Am overflowing joy!

I Am gratitude!

I Am freedom!

I Am allness!

I Am loving!

I Am lovable forever!

I Am in God!

I Am God's spirit creating through this body!

I Am a cocreator with God!

I Am awareness!

I Am selfless service and surrendered to the greatest good for all of creation!

Finish with the Closure

And so it is!

7

Suggested Hymn/Prayer

Here is a Hymn/Prayer that I suggest that
you sing or recite at least when
you wake up and/or before you go to sleep at
night or at any time during the day.

The tune to sing this is available on the website
www.justbelove.org on the CD, We R 1

I Am Loved, I Am Loving, I Am Lovable Forever.

I Am love, joy, appreciation, gratitude and peace,
I Am the bliss, oneness, beingness and okeness in all!

I Am loved, I Am loving, I Am lovable forever,
I'm the bliss, oneness, beingness and okeness in God!

Follow this with The Greatest Prayer!

The Greatest Prayer

Let us just be love,
Ho opono po no,

Namaste and
Peace be to all,
Glory to God in the highest!
Amen!

8

The Greatest Prayer

**This prayer is for all Higher Jihadis of Love to recite to any person, place, thing or situation,
because each has the same Essence of Spirit underlying it.**

1. Let Us Just Be Love!

This is an acronym for: Love's Eternal
Test Under Stress. Joyfully,
Unite, Share, Trust, Beautiful, Eternal, **LOVE!**
Love is Love Only, Victory Ensues.

2. Ho Opono Po No!

This is a Hawaian forgiveness and healing prayer, which means:
I'm sorry! Please forgive me! Thank you! I love you!

3. Namaste!

This is from Hindu philosophy and means:
"The Spirit in me honours the Spirit in you!"

4. Peace Be to All!

5. Gloria en Excelcis Deo!

Latin for: "Glory to God in the highest!"

5. Amen!
And so it is!

Think it! Feel it! Say it! Live it! Be it!
Peace be with you all ways!

9

Glossary

The meanings defined here are based on the perceptions and understanding of the author.

Alfa and Omega – The origin and the end of all creation.

Angel – A messenger from God, a positive inspiration, positive help from a person or positive intuition.

Ascension – The elevation of one's awareness and expression from a material plane of vibration, to a higher more spiritual vibrational level.

Being – A human being with seven vibrational bodies.

Bodies: Four lower vibrational: Physical, Emotional, Mental, Etheric. Three higher vibrational: Christ Self, Causal, I AM Presence.

Christself – the mediator between the I AM Presence- the essence of God – and the lower bodies, and the Causal body – around the I AM Presence where the good of the being is stored.

The Christ – the infinite and eternal child of God

A Christ – A human being that is fully aware that it is the peace, awareness and love of God experiencing creation and expanding it using a mortal body. Like Jesus and Gautama Buddha, we are parts of the body of The Christ.

Christian – A Christ in action, loving, caring and nurturing all of creation for the highest and greatest good of all.

Consciousness – An acute awareness of all states of being, material, non-material or spiritual.

Creation – the expression of all the ideas or concepts of God on whatever theme in forms that are tangible or not to the human senses.

Cross – A symbol of the interaction of energies. The vertical part represents spiritual energies while the horizontal part represents physical energies. If the long vertical part is upright then spiritual energies have predominance and more harmony is manifested.

Death – the surrender of the physical body by a living being to continue its spiritual evolution in spiritual dimensions until it is reborn in the material realm if that is its choice.

Decree – a command or order which elicits a response.

Disease – Disharmony in the mental emotional or spiritual actions of a being that results in dis ease or disfunction in the physical body.

Emotional body – The sheath of awareness where all the emotions of the being are stored.

Etheric Body – The sheath of the body where all negative experiences are recorded.

Fear – Future Events Appearing Real. A fantasy generated by negative emotions of low vibrations that trigger instinctual survival reactions that cause pain and suffering.

God – Goodness on demand, The source of all creation. Omniscient, Omnipotent and Omnipresent.

Great Central Sun – the origin of all the energies of creation.

Great White Brotherhood – A group of highly aware spiritual beings, who are dedicated to promoting harmony in all of creation according to the plan of the Creator source,

Heaven – A vibratory dimension of awareness in which a being is in complete harmony with all the aspects of creation it interacts with.

Helios and Vesta – The spiritual leaders of our solar system.

Hell – Opposite of Heaven.

Jesus – A manifestation of The Christ, who was the Avatar of the Piscean era and incarnated as Jeshua Ben Joseph.

Love – When pure and unconditional, it is the glue that permits different elements (vibrations) of creation, both living and nonliving, to unite, to manifest other aspects of creation of beauty harmony and wellbeing for all aspects of creation. It is the essence of God – the source of all creation. It is infinite, eternal, unchanging and unchangeable. Its forms include all the positive energies of God that uplift all of creation.

Master of Life – God, The Source of all life.

Mental Body – Thoughts and memories are processed and stored on this lower body.

Mortal mind - The mind associated with the human body that is governed by the ego.

Mind – This **M**ind is the infinite, eternal, spiritual mind of God that is a part of our spiritual nature as God's image and likeness.

Omniscient – All knowing.

Omnipotent – All powerful.

Omnipresent – Everywhere.

Power – Energies directed by Mind/Spirit.

Sacred Fire – Pure and powerful energy from God that can be directed by intention to neutralise or replace transitory conflictive behaviours or patterns with harmonious ones.

Sin – An acronym for Sensual Indulgence, which is ultimately detrimental to the wellbeing of the sinner or others. This occurs through any or all of one's thoughts, feelings, words and deeds.

Transmute – Change from one condition to another. Here it is used to change from the negative to the positive or bad to good.

Truth – Absolutely flawless expressions.

Wisdom – Truth tempered by experience and compassion.

Made in the USA
Middletown, DE
10 May 2023